In Spirit and Truth

In Spirit and Truth

A STUDY OF CHRISTIAN WORSHIP

DARREN CUSHMAN WOOD

North United Methodist Church • Indianapolis, IN

© 2023 North United Methodist Church, 3808 N. Meridian St., Indianapolis, IN 46208. NorthChurchIndy.com.

ISBN 978-1-7327761-5-9 (epub)
ISBN 978-1-7327761-6-6 (paperback)

The cover art comes from a small portion of one of the many beautiful banners throughout North United Methodist Church created by the late Doris Douglas, a long-time member, and other artists.

Biblical quotations from the New Revised Standard Version of the Bible, copyright © 1989 by the Division of Christian Education of the National Council of the Churches of Christ in the USA and used by permission.

Hymn quotations from The United Methodist Hymnal, copyright © 1989 by the United Methodist Publishing House and from The Faith We Sing, copyright © 2000 by Abingdon Press and used by permission.

Contents

Introduction   1

Part I. Main Body

1. How to Get Lit   5
2. How to Pray Aloud   13
3. How to Shake Hands   21
4. How to Eat and Drink   27
5. How to Pass the Plate   33
6. How to Say 'Amen'   39

    About the Author   45

Introduction

"Worship" is derived from a combination of two Old English words: weorth meaning "honor" or "worthiness," and scipe meaning "to create." When we worship we are creating honor for the one who is the focal point of the celebration.

For whom are we creating honor? It is not for ourselves or for a projection of our best intentions and highest aspirations. Worship is for God, whom we meet in Jesus Christ. Christ is the focus of our worship.

Creating honor takes some effort and energy, and so it is fitting that the word "liturgy" is derived from a Latin word that means "the work of the people." All of us — not just the preacher or the worship leaders — are actively involved in this weekly work of making honor for Christ.

The amazing thing about worship is that it makes us into God's people. If we let it, over time the intentional practice of worship shapes and reshapes our attitude and actions. Worship is not just something that happens. It is a deliberate activity that deepens and broadens our faith. We can call worship a spiritual discipline that we do together.

The irony is that the less we focus on ourselves in worship, the more we benefit from it. When we put the focus on the Triune God we are put into a right relationship with our Creator and Redeemer, who fulfills us and restores our right relationship with the rest of creation. Worship as a spiritual discipline benefits us when we are not the center of it.

I offer this definition of worship: Worship is the intentional, communal act of recentering our lives and our life together in the life of the Triune God.

There is a lot to unpack in that sentence, and certainly there are other ways to define worship. This study is based on the assumption that worship is:

1. a spiritual practice and not something we do by accident;
2. something we do together and not a solitary act;
3. something done in and through Jesus Christ, in whose Spirit we encounter God; and
4. by focusing on God we are renewed in all dimensions of our lives.

This study is designed to help you discover the benefits of worship by refocusing your attention on Jesus Christ as the center of worship.

We will explore the rituals of worship that seem small and may be taken for granted. Because worship forms us most through the things we do and not just through the words we say, the emphasis is on the practices of worship and their meanings, rather than the specific language or liturgies.

There are two major aspects of worship that this study does not address: reading scripture and preaching, and music. These have been omitted because each topic could be an entire study of its own. This study highlights other aspects of worship that are often overshadowed by preaching and music.

All scripture is taken from the New Revised Standard Version of the Bible, copyright 1989 by the Division of Christian

Education of the National Council of the Churches of Christ in the USA.

4

1. How to Get Lit

CENTERING

Take several long, slow breaths and imagine the Holy Spirit moving through your breathing, coming into the center of your being with God's light and removing from you the thoughts and concerns that distract you from God.

READINGS

Exodus 3:1-6[1]

Moses was taking care of the flock for his father-in-law, Jethro, Midian's priest. He led his flock out to the edge of the desert, and he came to God's mountain called Horeb. ²The Lord's messenger appeared to him in a flame of fire in the middle of a bush. Moses saw that the bush was in flames, but it didn't burn up. ³Then Moses said to himself, 'Let me check out this amazing sight and find out why the bush isn't burning up.' ⁴When the Lord saw that he was coming to look, God called to him out of the bush, "Moses, Moses!" Moses said, "I'm here. ⁵Then the Lord said, "Don't come any closer! Take off your sandals, because you are standing on holy ground." [6]He continued, "I am the God of your father, Abraham's God, Isaac's God, and Jacob's God. Moses hid his face because he was afraid to look at God.

John 1:1-5, 10-16

[1]In the beginning was the Word, and the Word was with God, and the Word was God. [2]The Word was with God in the beginning. [3]Everything came into being through the Word, and without the Word nothing came into being. What came into being [4]through the Word was life, and the life was the light for all people. [5]The light shines in the darkness, and the darkness doesn't extinguish the light.

[10]The light was in the world, and the world came into being through the light, but the world didn't recognize the light. [11]The light came to his own people, and his own people didn't welcome him. [12]But those who did welcome him, those who believed in his name, he authorized to become God's children, [13]born not from blood, nor from human desire or passion, but born from God. [14]The Word became flesh and made his home among us. We have seen his glory; glory like that of a father's only son, full of grace and truth. [15]John testified about him, crying out, "This is the one of whom I said, 'He who comes after me is greater than me because he existed before me.'" [16]From his fullness we have all received grace upon grace.

THE RITUAL: CALL TO WORSHIP

Over the centuries people have been called to worship by

the blowing of a shofar, the ringing of church bells, and the blast of electric guitars.

How do you prepare for worship? Choose the ones that are part of your normal routine:

___ Pray earlier in the week or early on Sunday morning

___ Visit with friends in the hallway

___ Attend Sunday school

___ Greet guests

___ Help with the set-up or ushering

___ Read the Scripture passages for that Sunday

___ Read or sing the hymns for that Sunday

___ Listen to the prelude

___ Bookmark the hymns

___ Read through the bulletin

Which ones do you need to start doing to enrich your worship experience?

THE MEANING OF THE RITUAL: CALL TO WORSHIP

Worship begins with a choice — but not ours. God chooses to invite all of us to worship. God plants the desire in our hearts, creates the opportunity, and gives us the resources of liturgy and leadership to worship. And so, worship begins with

God's invitation that is expressed through the call to worship. God calls us to move (mentally and physically) from our everyday concerns and routines into God's time and space.

There are several different things we can do to prepare to accept God's invitation. We connect with one another in the hallway, and we learn about the ministries of the church through the announcements. (These joys, opportunities, and concerns often come into worship through the various prayers and rituals of dedication that are done later in the service.)

Then we prepare to connect with God by centering our hearts and minds with the music of an organ prelude, a choral introit, or a praise band medley. These "horizontal" and "vertical" routines prepare us to orient every dimension of our lives toward the praise of God.

How was Moses called into the presence of God?

How does worship help us enter into the experience of the "holy?"

Moses was told to remove his shoes because he was standing on holy ground. What do we need to "remove" in order to worship?

THE RITUAL: RECEIVING THE LIGHT OF CHRIST

Acts 20:8 is the first reference to candles being used in evening worship, possibly as a midnight vigil.

Candles were first used around the altar, and it was after A.D. 1000 that they were placed on the altar.

In Anglican circles, in 1547 Edward VI ordered that two

lights adorn the high altar to symbolize Christ as the true light, but in Eastern Orthodoxy seven candles were the tradition.

Other forms of lights have been used, such as a perpetual flame in front of the tabernacle containing the communion elements and the lighting of the Paschal (Easter) candle for the Easter sunrise vigil.

What are your expectations of worship (both at your own church as well as at another church)?

THE MEANING OF THE RITUAL: RECEIVING THE LIGHT OF CHRIST

Receiving the light of Christ at the beginning of a worship service symbolizes that the presence of Christ is essential for worship. Jesus Christ is the center of Christian worship, and the presence of the Spirit of Christ makes the gathering an encounter with the divine.

His presence is essential for four reasons:

1. It is through Christ the Word as the second person of the Trinity that we enter into God's presence and participate in God's being (John 1:1; we become "partakers of the divine nature" as it says in 2 Peter 1:4). A couple of years ago, our confirmation class gave the best description of this: Christ is the window to God.
2. Christ reveals the truth about the world we live in, both its beauty and its brokenness. He is the light that shines on all people and gives life to all creation, and when we worship in the Spirit of Christ we can see the world from God's perspective (John 1:3-4).
3. The presence of Christ unites all believers in worship

(John 1:12).

4. Christ fulfills the desires and gives purpose to our lives. We encounter Christ in worship and his presence renews us. (John 1:16).

In all these ways, we encounter Christ in worship. This encounter "ignites" our lives with faith, truth, hope. and love.

And still, we are not the focus of worship. Worship is not centered on the charismatic personality of a leader. It is not organized around an ideology, nor is it the glorification of one particular culture.

And yet worship is always a cultural expression. We do not escape from the world through worship because it is inevitable that we use the language and symbols of society to worship. Worship, therefore, is always a mix of affirming and transcending our particular cultures.

This dynamic is found in the Incarnation. "The Word became flesh and made his home among us" means that Christ makes God known through the diversity of human expressions in worship while enabling us to go beyond the limitations of those expressions. When our worship becomes fixated on one particular form it becomes idolatry. God delights in the diversity of human expressions in worship because God resides in these expressions without being contained by them.

How does seeing Christ as the center of worship reshape our thoughts and feelings about ourselves and the world around us?

What would happen if Jesus did not show up for our worship?

CENTRAL WORSHIP QUESTIONS

Why do you worship?

What does it mean to "encounter Christ" in worship?

OTHER 'LITURGIES' THAT SHAPE US

American Christianity has been influenced by a variety of cultural dynamics that we often take for granted. In particular, two things have an impact on mainline Protestant worship: rationalism and consumerism.

Rational thinking and the scientific method have shaped our definition of truth and how we define reality. Our consumer-driven economy permeates every aspect of society by reducing relationships to transactions and manufacturing desires.

Consider these questions:

What role should human reason play in worship? What are the limits of reason in worship?

In what ways is Christian worship shaped by consumerism? What other things replace Christ as the center of worship (even when we use the language about Christ in worship)?

As part of your personal preparation for worship, light a candle and use it as a focal point for meditation. Read Psalm 63.

2. How to Pray Aloud

CENTERING

Recite aloud the following prayer as a way to center your thoughts and feelings on God:

Lord, open my/our heart(s) and mind(s)
by the power of your Holy Spirit,
that, as the Scriptures are read
and your Word proclaimed,
I/we may hear with joy what you say to me/us today.
Amen.

READINGS

Joel 1:13-15; 2:26-32

1:13Put on sackcloth and lament, you priests; wail, you ministers of the altar. Come, pass the night in sackcloth, you ministers of my God! Grain-offering and drink-offering are withheld from the house of your God. ¹⁴Sanctify a fast, call a solemn assembly. Gather the elders and all the inhabitants of the land to the house of the Lord your God, and cry out to the Lord. ¹⁵Alas for the day! For the day of the Lord is near, and as destruction from the Almighty it comes.

²:²⁶You shall eat in plenty and be satisfied, and praise the name of the Lord your God, who has dealt wondrously with you. And my people shall never again be put to shame. ²⁷You shall know that I am in the midst of Israel, and that I, the Lord, am your God and there is no other. And my people shall never again be put to shame. ²⁸Then afterwards I will pour out my spirit on all flesh; your sons and your daughters shall prophesy; your old men shall dream dreams; and your young men shall see visions. ²⁹Even on the male and female slaves, in those days, I will pour out my spirit. ³⁰I will show portents in the heavens and on the earth, blood and fire and columns of smoke. ³¹The sun shall be turned to darkness, and the moon to blood, before the great and terrible day of the Lord comes. ³²Then everyone who calls on the name of the Lord shall be saved; for in Mount Zion and in Jerusalem there shall be those who escape, as the Lord has said, and among the survivors shall be those whom the Lord calls.

Acts 4:23-31

²³After they were released, they went to their friends and reported what the chief priests and the elders had said to them. ²⁴When they heard it, they raised their voices together to God and said, 'Sovereign Lord, who made the heaven and the earth, the sea, and everything in them, ²⁵it is you who said by the Holy Spirit through our ancestor David, your servant: "Why

did the Gentiles rage, and the peoples imagine vain things? [26]The kings of the earth took their stand, and the rulers have gathered together against the Lord and against his Messiah." [27]For in this city, in fact, both Herod and Pontius Pilate, with the Gentiles and the peoples of Israel, gathered together against your holy servant Jesus, whom you anointed, [28]to do whatever your hand and your plan had predestined to take place. [29]And now, Lord, look at their threats, and grant to your servants to speak your word with all boldness, [30]while you stretch out your hand to heal, and signs and wonders are performed through the name of your holy servant , Jesus.' [31]When they had prayed, the place in which they were gathered together was shaken; and they were all filled with the Holy Spirit and spoke the word of God with boldness.

THE RITUAL: COMMUNAL PRAYERS

Our worship is full of a variety of prayers that are said in unison or responsively. Each prayer functions in a different way, but all are essential parts of worship. Indeed, one could define the entire worship experience as a communal act of prayer.

Each type of prayer has its own history and development. Christian prayers in worship are rooted in the Jewish Berakah (Hebrew, "blessing").

The litany, as a style of prayer using short, fixed responses, originated in Antioch in the late fourth century.

The first time we see a full-fledged prayer of thanksgiving for communion is in A.D. 215 by Hippolytus.

At the beginning of the 20th century Catholic scholars sought to reclaim an ancient understanding of worship and recover ancient forms of corporate prayer. This became known as the Liturgical Movement, and after World War II it influenced Protestant scholars who revised the Great Thanksgiving (the prayer for communion) in mainline denominations.

Which of the following communal prayers is most meaningful to you?
___Prayer for Illumination
___Prayers of Intercession
___Prayer of Confession
___The Great Thanksgiving (communion)
___The Thanksgiving over the Water (baptism)

THE MEANING OF THE RITUAL

Five things happen when the church prays together:

1. The church acts as a mediator between God and the world.

One of the roles of the church is to act as a representative in both directions. As part of the priestly function of the church, we express the needs and aspirations of humanity to God, and we share God's message to the world (I Peter 2:4-5).

2. Praying together recalls and enacts God's story.

"Prayer enacts an entire cosmology," according to theologian James Smith, "because implicit in the very act of prayer is a [way of understanding] the God-world relationship."[2]

Our prayers remind us that we are a part of a larger story of God's creative and redeeming work, and that we are a part of the larger history of God's people.

3. Praying together expresses human pathos.

In corporate prayer, we bring the fullness and diversity of the human experience into the sacred dimension of worship.

According to theologian Don Saliers, liturgy is a "mutual dialogue with God's self-communication."

An authentic dialogue conveys the aspirations and the sufferings of humanity. In doing this, liturgy "lifts up all that is human to the transforming power of communal life animated in the Spirit."[3]

4. Corporate prayer forms individual character.

When we pray together we learn how to live as disciples of Jesus Christ. Like children learning how to speak from hearing their parents, Christians are taught through communal experiences of prayer.

5. Praying together shapes the church.

The fellowship is deepened when we lift one another up in prayer. The mission is expanded when we pray for the world. Prayer is the channel through which the Spirit of Christ develops the spiritual unity of believers and empowers the church not to conform to the world.

In Ezra, the people gathered in the Temple to fast and pray together. How might these experiences have shaped their collective identity? Their personal self-understanding?

Review the types of corporate prayers. How does each one of them shape the church's identity and an individual's self-understanding?

Prayer for Illumination
Prayers of Intercession
Prayer of Confession
The Great Thanksgiving (communion)
The Thanksgiving over the Water (baptism)

In Acts, how did praying together express:
1. a way of remembering;
2. human desires and emotions, and
3. the church as the mediator between God and humanity?

Do our prayers in worship adequately express human aspirations and suffering?

CENTRAL WORSHIP QUESTION

Why worship together?

OTHER 'LITURGIES' THAT SHAPE US

We live in a highly individualistic culture, which has become more so over the past 40 years. In what ways does individualism influence:
- Whether we worship or not?
- How we participate in worship?
- Our expectations about worship and its leaders?

THIS WEEK

Every day this week begin by reading one of the following Prayers for Illumination:

O Fire Divine, go through my heart.
O Light Eternal, illuminate my soul.
Reveal the peace and power of Christ
in our singing and our silence
so that we can bear witness
to the hope of heaven here on earth.

Amen.

Spirit of the Living God,
free our minds from error,
teach our hearts the living words of Jesus,
and inspire our lips to share the Good News,
in the name of the blessed Holy Trinity. Amen.

Living God,
breathe life into our hearts and minds
through the reading of scripture
that we may be equipped for every good work,
to the glory of Jesus Christ, your Word. Amen.

Read Psalm 80.

Conclude this daily devotion by praying one of the following prayers of confession:

Forgive us, Lord Jesus,
for our stubborn resistance
that scoffs at your way,
our comfortable arrogance
that rejects your truth,
and our lazy faith that avoids your life.
Touch our souls and trouble our hearts
until we are made new in the Spirit. Amen.

God of loyal love,
we confess that we have
replaced your praise with our complaints,
rejected your glory for our pride,

resisted your will for our way.
We have worshiped ourselves
and dishonored your name.
Forgive us and help us to be loyal to you,
through Jesus Christ our Lord. Amen.

We confess, O God,
that we have relied on ourselves,
we have used others,
and we have ignored you.
Destroy our sinful illusions,
and sustain us in the reality of your grace
that we may bear the fruit
of mercy, justice and peace
to a hurting world;
in the name of Jesus Christ we pray. Amen.

3. How to Shake Hands

CENTERING

Look at your hands. Think back over the past 24 hours of all the people you touched with your hands and all the tasks you did with your hands. With your palms turned upward, pray for those persons and tasks, asking for God's blessing and consecration on them.

READINGS

Micah 4:1-7

[1]In days to come the mountain of the Lord's house shall be established as the highest of the mountains, and shall be raised up above the hills. Peoples shall stream to it, [2]and many nations shall come and say: 'Come, let us go up to the mountain of the Lord, to the house of the God of Jacob; that he may teach us his ways and that we may walk in his paths.' For out of

Zion shall go forth instruction, and the word of the Lord from Jerusalem. ³He shall judge between many peoples, and shall arbitrate between strong nations far away; they shall beat their swords into ploughshares, and their spears into pruning hooks; nation shall not lift up sword against nation, neither shall they learn war anymore; ⁴but they shall all sit under their own vines and under their own fig trees, and no one shall make them afraid; for the mouth of the Lord of hosts has spoken. ⁵For all the peoples walk, each in the name of its god, but we will walk in the name of the Lord our God forever and ever. ⁶On that day, says the Lord, I will assemble the lame and gather those who have been driven away, and those whom I have afflicted. ⁷The lame I will make the remnant, and those who were cast off, a strong nation; and the Lord will reign over them in Mount Zion now and forevermore.

Romans 16:16-20

¹⁶Greet one another with a holy kiss. All the churches of Christ greet you. ¹⁷I urge you, brothers and sisters, to keep an eye on those who cause dissensions and offences, in opposition to the teaching that you have learned; avoid them. ¹⁸For such people do not serve our Lord Christ, but their own appetites, and by smooth talk and flattery they deceive the hearts of the simple minded. ¹⁹For while your obedience is known to all, so that I rejoice over you, I want you to be wise in what is good, and guileless in what is evil. ²⁰The God of peace will shortly crush Satan under your feet. The grace of our Lord Jesus Christ be with you.

THE RITUAL: PASSING THE PEACE

The holy kiss and other signs of peace were associated

with the offertory. Usually it was done at the end of the Prayer of Consecration and before the Eucharist was celebrated. It also concluded the consecration of bishops as a symbol of unity.

How do you pass the peace? (circle all that apply):

"Peace of Christ" or "Good morning"

Stay in your place or move around

Greet the people you know or seek out those you don't know

THE MEANING OF THE RITUAL

The passing of the peace represents two gifts of Christ.

One, we pass the peace to symbolize our unity as the followers of Jesus. Traditionally it was done right before the offering of the communion elements to fulfill Jesus' command to reconcile with one's enemy before making an offering at the altar (see Matthew 5:23-24).

Two, the ritual is a symbolic forerunner of the hope of universal peace.

What is Micah's vision of society?

How do we extend the signs of peace beyond worship and into everyday life?

Paul alluded to "dissensions and offenses" in the church. What kinds of problems in the church make it difficult for the passing of the peace to be an authentic sign of our unity?

How might the ritual be a part of the healing and restoration of a congregation?

How is Christian unity a gift from Christ, and at the same time a command of Christ?

CENTRAL WORSHIP QUESTIONS

What can we do to invite and welcome more people to worship with us?

In what ways can you help someone who is new to our worship to be fully included?

OTHER 'LITURGIES' THAT SHAPE US

Our society is deeply divided over cultural and political issues. The advent of social media has accelerated our tribal inclinations and tempts us to stay in our echo chambers. At the same time, we are an increasingly isolated and lonely people.

What divides people in our society?

How can the church be an alternative to these divisions?

Why do people isolate themselves?

How can the church help people overcome their isolation?

THIS WEEK

Get a copy of the prayer requests in your church for the

week. Each day, pray for these persons and needs and conclude with a "caim" prayer, a traditional Celtic prayer for those in need:

Circle them, Lord.
Keep comfort near and discouragement afar.
Keep peace within and turmoil out. Amen.[4]

4. How to Eat and Drink

CENTERING

Recite the "Sanctus," which is one of the responses in the Great Thanksgiving for communion:

> Holy, holy, holy Lord,
> God of power and might,
> heaven and earth are full of your glory.
> Hosanna in the highest.
> Blessed is he who comes
> in the name of the Lord.
> Hosanna in the highest.

READINGS

Exodus 13:1-10[5]

[1]The Lord said to Moses: [2]Dedicate to me all your oldest chil-

dren. Each first offspring from any Israelite womb belongs to me, whether human or animal. ³Moses said to the people, "Remember this day, which is the day that you came out of Egypt, out of the place you were slaves, because the Lord acted with power to bring you out of there. No leavened bread may be eaten. ⁴Today, in the month of Abib, you are going to leave. ⁵The Lord will bring you to the land of the Canaanites, the Hittites, the Amorites, the Hivites, and the Jebusites. It is the land that the Lord promised your ancestors to give to you, a land full of milk and honey. You should perform this ritual in this month. ⁶You must eat unleavened bread for seven days. The seventh day is a festival to the Lord. ⁷Only unleavened bread should be eaten for seven days. No leavened bread and no yeast should be seen among you in your whole country. ⁸You should explain to your child on that day, 'It's because of what the Lord did for me when I came out of Egypt.' ⁹"It will be a sign on your hand and a reminder on your forehead so that you will often discuss the Lord's instruction, for the Lord brought you out of Egypt with great power. ¹⁰So you should follow this regulation at its appointed time every year.

I Corinthians 11:23-29

²³I received a tradition from the Lord, which I also handed on to you: on the night on which he was betrayed, the Lord Jesus took bread. ²⁴After giving thanks, he broke it and said, "This is my body, which is for you; do this to remember me." ²⁵He did the same thing with the cup, after they had eaten, saying, "This cup is the new covenant in my blood. Every time you drink it, do this to remember me." ²⁶Every time you eat this bread and drink this cup, you broadcast the death of the Lord until he comes. ²⁷This is why those who eat the bread or drink the cup

of the Lord inappropriately will be guilty of the Lord's body and blood. [28]Each individual should test himself or herself, and eat from the bread and drink from the cup in that way. [29]Those who eat and drink without correctly understanding the body are eating and drinking their own judgment.

THE SACRAMENT

The Lord's Supper (also called "communion" and "the Eucharist") has a long and complex history of development.

From the beginning it was a combination of Jewish and Greek elements that the church used to express in a new way that Jesus Christ was the center of their communal life.

From Judaism, the early Christians adapted the blessing of Birkat ha-Mazon and the bread. From Greek dinner parties, they adapted the libation of wine.

At first the celebration was a full communal meal, but over time it became a separate ritualistic meal of wine and bread.

Fast forward to the 18th century. John Wesley encouraged the Methodists to practice "constant communion." In was his desire that the Methodists partake every Sunday. But due to a shortage of ministers, American Methodists took it about four times a year. Over the past 40 years we have adopted the practice of receiving communion on the first Sunday of the month.

How do you prefer to receive communion?
_____kneeling
_____standing
_____sitting in a pew
_____intinction (dipping the bread into the chalice)
_____in separate cups
_____every Sunday

_____once a month
_____a few times a year on special occasions

THE MEANING OF THE SACRAMENT

Unlike the previous sessions, this section is not called "the meaning of the ritual" but "the meaning of the sacrament" because the Lord's Supper is a sacrament.

A sacrament is a type of ritual that we believe was started by Christ and is a means of God's grace.

With other Protestants, we believe there are two sacraments: baptism and the Lord's Supper. Baptism is an initiatory sacrament and the Lord's Supper is for the ongoing edification of believers.

As a reliable channel of God's grace, communion has more than one meaning. In Charles Wesley's hymnal for the Lord's Supper (1745), he divided the songs according to stages of time. The Lord's Supper tells us something about our relationship with Christ in the past, the present, and the future. In addition, the sacrament has meaning both for the individual and the church.

Complete the accompanying chart to understand the six dimensions of communion. Look up the scripture references and the hymns to discover the meaning of each category:

	For the Individual	*For the Church*
Past	Forgiveness of Sins 1 Cor. 11:24-25 "There is a Fountain Filled with Blood"	Remembering the Saints Hebrews 12:1 "For All the Saints"
Present	Nourishing the New Life in Christ John 6:35 "Come, Sinners, to the Gospel Feast" "Fill My Cup, Lord"	United in the Spirit Ephesians 4:1-6 1 Cor. 11:17-34 "Draw Us in the Spirit's Tether" "One Bread, One Body"
Future	Hope of Eternal Life Jude 20-21 "O the Depth of Love Divine," vv. 3-4	Hope of the Reign of God Revelation 21:1-8 "This Is the Feast of Victory"

Which of these six meanings is the most familiar to you?

Which one is a new perspective for you?

Which ones are the most meaningful for you?

CENTRAL WORSHIP QUESTION

In the first session, we described how Jesus Christ is the center of worship. The sacrament of the Lord's Supper raises questions about the relationship between Christ and culture. Jesus Christ is universal and eternal, but the sacrament celebrating him is always performed with the stuff of a specific culture (bread, wine, language, etc.).

When does a worship service cease to be focused on Christ, and instead the particular cultural expressions take center stage?

OTHER 'LITURGIES' THAT SHAPE US

The Eucharist expresses that the church lives by a different set of values from the world. The sacrament forms the church into a "countercultural community."

Using the chart in the above section, identify what you see in society as the opposite of each dimension of the Lord's Supper.

THIS WEEK

If you read this before celebrating the Lord's Supper, read I Corinthians 11:27-9 in preparation for the sacrament.

Examine your life and what you need to change or ask forgiveness for as you get ready to receive communion.

5. How to Pass the Plate

CENTERING

Read or sing the doxology:

Praise God, from whom all blessings flow;
Praise him, all creatures here below;
Praise him above, ye heavenly host;
Praise Father, Son, and Holy Ghost. Amen.

Then count the blessings God has given you this week.

READINGS

Ezra 3:1-7

[1]When the seventh month came, and the Israelites were in the towns, the people gathered together in Jerusalem. [2]Then Jeshua, son of Jozadak, with his fellow priests, and Zerubbabel,

son of Shealtiel with his kin, set out to build the altar of the God of Israel, to offer burnt offerings on it, as prescribed in the law of Moses the man of God. ³They set up the altar on its foundation, because they were in dread of the neighboring peoples, and they offered burnt offerings upon it to the Lord, morning and evening. ⁴And they kept the festival of booths, as prescribed, and offered the daily burnt offerings by number according to the ordinance, as required for each day, ⁵and after that the regular burnt offerings, the offerings at the new moon and at all the sacred festivals of the Lord, and the offerings of everyone who made a freewill offering to the Lord. ⁶From the first day of the seventh month they began to offer burnt offerings to the Lord. But the foundation of the temple of the Lord was not yet laid. ⁷So they gave money to the masons and the carpenters, and food, drink, and oil to the Sidonians and the Tyrians to bring cedar trees from Lebanon to the sea, to Joppa, according to the grant that they had from King Cyrus of Persia.

2 Corinthians 9:6-15

⁶The point is this: the one who sows sparingly will also reap sparingly, and the one who sows bountifully will also reap bountifully. ⁷Each of you must give as you have made up your mind, not reluctantly or under compulsion, for God loves a cheerful giver. ⁸And God is able to provide you with every blessing in abundance, so that by always having enough of everything, you may share abundantly in every good work. ⁹As it is written, 'He scatters abroad, he gives to the poor; his righteousness endures forever.' ¹⁰He who supplies seed to the sower and bread for food will supply and multiply your seed for sowing and increase the harvest of your righteousness. ¹¹You will be enriched in every way for your great generosity, which will

produce thanksgiving to God through us; [12]for the rendering of this ministry not only supplies the needs of the saints but also overflows with many thanksgivings to God. [13]Through the testing of this ministry you glorify God by your obedience to the confession of the gospel of Christ and by the generosity of your sharing with them and with all others, [14]while they long for you and pray for you because of the surpassing grace of God that he has given you. [15]Thanks be to God for his indescribable gift!

THE RITUAL

Collections have been linked with worship from the very beginning, with various offerings on altars and with the sharing of possessions in the early church.

Traditionally the offering came immediately before the prayer of consecration for the Lord's Supper because it was the presentation of the elements to be used in the sacrament. However, some traditions do not include an offering in the worship service, such as Mormon services and some contemporary "Seeker" services.

What are your earliest memories of giving to the church?

THE MEANING OF THE RITUAL

The traditional place of the offering before the Lord's Supper reminds us that our giving is a grateful response to the gift of Jesus Christ for our salvation. The offering also represented gratitude for the gifts of creation, as represented in the presentation of the bread and wine.

In addition to gratitude, the collection symbolizes our dedication to the way of Christ. Our gifts are consecrated by the Holy Spirit to be used for God's mission, and through the Spirit they become a part of Christ giving himself for the redemption of the world.

Why was the construction of an altar necessary for the re-establishment of the nation in Ezra?

Altars were built in the Old Testament on sites where people had had an encounter with God so that one could meet God again and again in that place. Altars "regularized a theophany," so to speak, by making an offering. Why is it important for us to make generosity a routine part of our lives?

What is the relationship between generosity and thanksgiving in 2 Corinthians 9?

How does giving require us to trust God?

CENTRAL WORSHIP QUESTION

Why is giving a part of worship? (Choose any that apply to you and rank them in order of importance to you.)

"The offering symbolizes....
___ my gratitude for God's blessings."
___ my commitment to God's mission."
___ my support for my church family."
___ the submission of my life to God."

OTHER 'LITURGIES' THAT SHAPE US

In "The Paradox of Generosity," Christian Smith and Hilary Davidson describe the beliefs of ungenerous Americans that they interviewed:

"Personal autonomy, self-preservation, and rugged individualism are key and sacred concepts in the vocabulary of the ungenerous people we interviewed.

"Devotion to self-interest is the most pervasive thread woven throughout our interviews....it is a thread intertwined with the fear of falling off the middle-class track of security. This clearly gives rise to a complex of stress, anxiety, insecurity, and banality.

"We find consistent evidence that ungenerous lifestyles associate with an apathy riddled by anxiety. Our interviews with Americans who do not practice generosity reveal that they are deeply unsettled by individual and social problems. Yet they do not think they have any obligation to respond, and even if they do, they feel inadequate to make a difference without sacrificing their ability to care for their own needs...They imagine other people as restrictions on their autonomy. Self-preservation and financial security are the main standards by which ungenerous Americans assess their lives. This approach thus stokes an anxiety that at worst is soothed by apathy and a withdrawal from concerns beyond one's own individual concerns, and at best results in some intermittent caring, volunteering, and financial generosity.[6]

What dynamics in society foster this worldview?

What do we say, sing and do in worship that promotes an alternative worldview of generosity?

THIS WEEK

Read Psalm 50. Reflect on three dimensions of generosity in your life:

1. Emotional generosity — How am I giving emotional support to others?
2. Timely generosity — How am I sharing my time and talents with others?
3. Financial generosity — How am I contributing financially to the work of God?

Set one challenging but realistic goal for yourself in each of these three areas of generosity.

6. How to Say 'Amen'

CENTERING

Read the following blessing as God saying this to you. Substitute your name wherever there is a "you."

"The Lord bless you and keep you;
The Lord make his face to shine upon you,
and be gracious to you;
The Lord lift up his countenance upon you,
and give you peace." (Numbers 6:24-6)

READINGS

Nehemiah 8:1-6

¹All the people gathered together into the square before the Water Gate. They told the scribe Ezra to bring the book of the law of Moses, which the Lord had given to Israel. ²Accord-

ingly, the priest Ezra brought the law before the assembly, both men and women and all who could hear with understanding. This was on the first day of the seventh month. ³He read from it facing the square before the Water Gate from early morning until midday, in the presence of the men and the women and those who could understand; and the ears of all the people were attentive to the book of the law. ⁴The scribe Ezra stood on a wooden platform that had been made for the purpose; and beside him stood Mattithiah, Shema, Anaiah, Uriah, Hilkiah, and Maaseiah on his right hand; and Pedaiah, Mishael, Malchijah, Hashum, Hash-baddanah, Zechariah, and Meshullam on his left hand. ⁵And Ezra opened the book in the sight of all the people, for he was standing above all the people; and when he opened it, all the people stood up. ⁶Then Ezra blessed the Lord, the great God, and all the people answered, 'Amen, Amen,' lifting up their hands. Then they bowed their heads and worshipped the Lord with their faces to the ground.

Mark 14:18-30

¹⁸And when they had taken their places and were eating, Jesus said, 'Truly I tell you, one of you will betray me, one who is eating with me.' ¹⁹They began to be distressed and to say to him one after another, 'Surely, not I?' ²⁰He said to them, 'It is one of the 12, one who is dipping bread into the bowl with me. ²¹For the Son of Man goes as it is written of him, but woe to that one by whom the Son of Man is betrayed! It would have been better for that one not to have been born.' ²²While they were eating, he took a loaf of bread, and after blessing it he broke it, gave it to them, and said, 'Take; this is my body.' ²³Then he took a cup, and after giving thanks he gave it to them, and all of them drank from it. ²⁴He said to them, 'This is my blood of the

covenant, which is poured out for many. ²⁵Truly I tell you, I will never again drink of the fruit of the vine until that day when I drink it new in the kingdom of God.' ²⁶When they had sung the hymn, they went out to the Mount of Olives. ²⁷And Jesus said to them, 'You will all become deserters; for it is written, "I will strike the shepherd, and the sheep will be scattered." ²⁸But after I am raised up, I will go before you to Galilee.' ²⁹Peter said to him, 'Even though all become deserters, I will not.' ³⁰Jesus said to him, 'Truly I tell you, this day, this very night, before the cock crows twice, you will deny me three times.'

THE RITUAL: THE BENEDICTION

Benediction comes from two Latin words, "bene" meaning "well," and "dicere" meaning "speak." The benediction is a "good word," as the last words of worship. A benediction can be a blessing and/or a charge. The benediction can be spoken or sung.

A blessing is a pronouncement that conveys approval and empowerment. When you are blessed, you are chosen and equipped with power and authority from the one giving you the blessing.

Sometimes the benediction is comprised of a charge to the people as well as a blessing. A charge is a pronouncement for the worshipper to put their faith into practice in the coming week.

MEANING OF THE RITUAL: THE BENEDICTION

Whether it is a benediction or a blessing, it ends with "amen." Amen is a Hebrew term that connotes being firm or faithful.

In addition to "amen" appearing in scripture, it is also translated as "verily" and "truly." The basic idea of amen is "let it be so" or "may it happen as said." Thus, one says in response to a divine pronouncement, "amen."

On the night of Jesus' Last Supper he says it three times:

And when they had taken their places and were eating, Jesus said, 'Truly ["amen"] I tell you, one of you will betray me, one who is eating with me'.... Truly ["amen"] I tell you, I will never again drink of the fruit of the vine until that day when I drink it new in the kingdom of God'.... Jesus said to him, 'Truly ["amen"] I tell you, this day, this very night, before the cock crows twice, you will deny me three times.' (Mark 14:18, 25, 30)

In other words, Jesus is saying, "So be it that I am going to be betrayed, abandoned, and killed." His amen expresses his willing commitment to the tragic steps that enact our salvation.

And so, it is fitting that we end our worship by saying amen as a response to Jesus' amen. When we say amen at the end of our worship we are affirming our desire and pledging our commitment to live out the beliefs we have said in worship. We are saying, "Let everything we have said and sung in worship become a reality for the rest of our lives."

When have you been blessed by an experience of worship?

When has worship challenged you to serve in the name of Jesus?

How does worship sustain your calling to serve?

What visions of God's peace and justice do we see and

hear in worship that we need to say "so be it" ("amen") come Monday morning?

CENTRAL WORSHIP QUESTION

Examine what you are doing and thinking at the end of worship. When the service comes to an end and the minister is giving the benediction, I tend to:

_____ look at my watch to see how long the service was
_____ get my stuff together so I can get out of the pew quickly
_____ start talking to those around me
_____ close my eyes and pray along with the minister
_____ raise my hands in praise or open my hands in ready service

OTHER 'LITURGIES' THAT SHAPE US

In his book "The Cynical Society," Jeffrey Goldfarb describes how our political culture is saturated with cynicism that is a form of despair operating under the guise of being insightful about the sinful foibles of leaders.

Cynicism promotes an evasion of personal responsibility by giving us false excuses. Cynicism discourages cooperation and undermines constructive criticism.

Consider these questions:

When have you heard examples of cynicism about worship?

How do the liturgies and music of worship offer a vision of society that opposes cynicism?

THIS WEEK

Find one person that you can bless with your words of encouragement and show of support.

---

[1] "Common English Bible" translation.

[2] "Desiring the Kingdom: Worship, Worldview and Cultural Formation," (Baker Acadic, 2009), 193.

[3] "Worship in Theology" (Abingdon, 1994), 26.

[4] From "Celtic Daily Prayer," The Northumbria Community, Collins, 2000.

[5] "Common English Bible" translation.

[6] (University of Oxford Press, 2014), 119-20, 177.

About the Author

Darren Cushman Wood is the senior pastor of North United Methodist Church in Indianapolis, Indiana. He has served small and large, rural and urban United Methodist churches for over 30 years. He is a graduate of the University of Evansville and Union Theological Seminary.

He is the author of two books, hymns, and numerous articles. He is an adjunct professor of labor studies at Indiana University. He is married to Ginny and as of this writing they have three adult children and one grandchild.

www.ingramcontent.com/pod-product-compliance
Lightning Source LLC
LaVergne TN
LVHW021626080426
835510LV00019B/2771